KIKUO (1996.12.04.M.#d7_08)
(RECLINING WOO-MAN), 1996

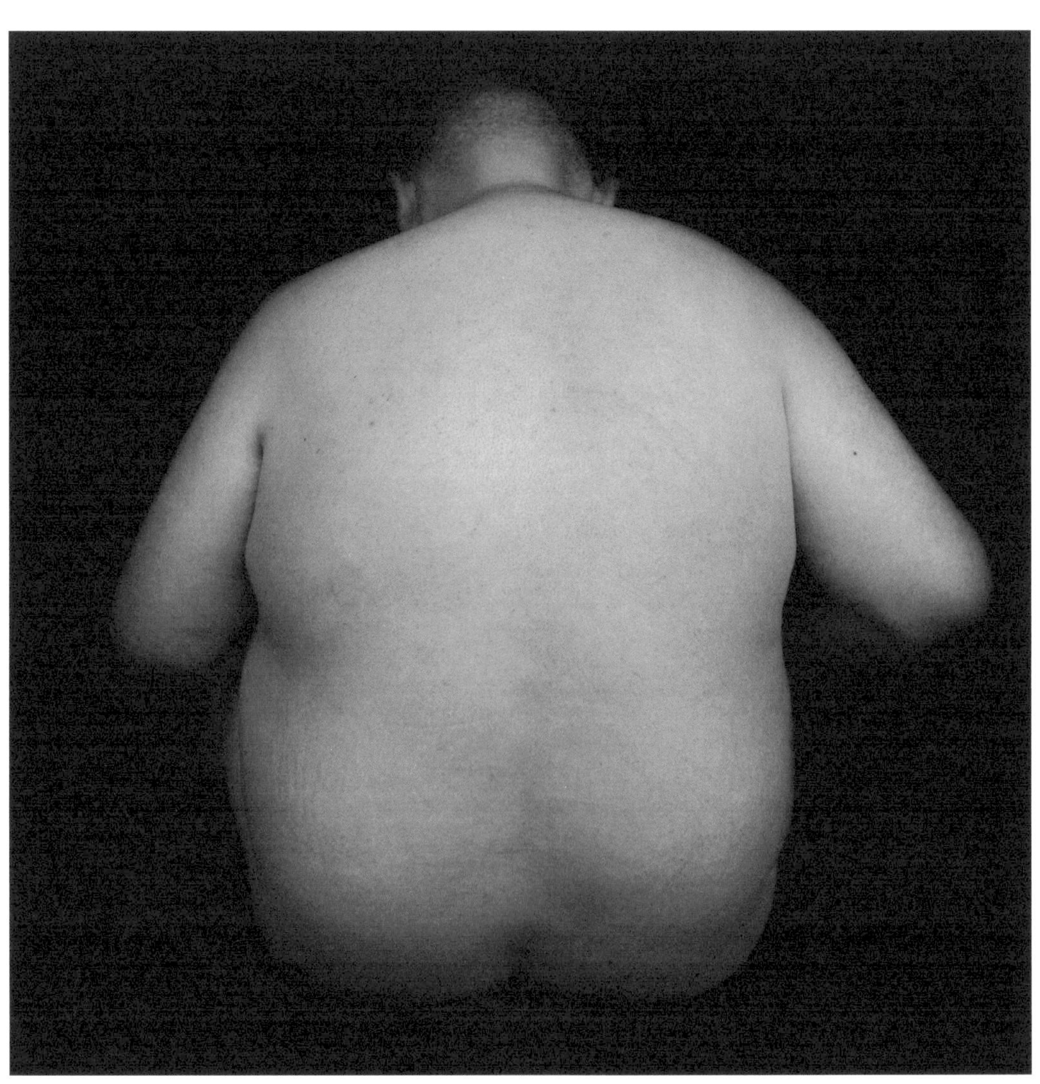

RYUDAI TAKANO

キクオ

KIKUO

(RECLINING WOO—MAN)

Do we reproduce the world, or transform it? Do we record the world as it has been shown to us, or permit the camera to reveal new ways of looking, thinking or acting? This is a central question for photography: production or reproduction? A bringing into being, or the world as it is? Photography alters what we think we know: perspectives appear different, and the normal becomes strange. The beautiful, too, might switch places with the ordinary or the abject; our values might be tested and challenged, and our opinions overturned.

It was in Paris in November 2017 that I first saw Ryudai Takano's *Kikuo (Reclining Woo-Man)*, his bulging yet fragile body an unexpected mixture of the familiar and the unfamiliar. His comfort is recognizable, and his indifference confronts. A year later, my experience of another of Takano's photographs, *How to Contact a Man*, confirmed it: a transformation through photography; a challenge to the real. In the city of Edouard Manet's *Olympia*, I felt its impact strong: it is a mirror, like that great critique of representation, myth and fantasy.

Where painting had been a space of fancy, Manet brought the nude's unvarnished reality into the image: his model, Victorine Meurent, returns the gaze, constructing a scene no longer of voyeurism, but exchange. Takano, I think, suspects something in the photographic: that it is used to construct airbrushed fantasies and tidy fictions. He has set out to show the world: one part of this will be to make the male body visible.

Kikuo has a fleshy heft, a scale and form that fills the frame. And yet he rests casually, with a lightness that moves from a curved pose to a reflective slumber. His scale does not diminish the sense of fragility, a quality that we associate more readily with the feminine. In fact, the body of the reclining *Woo-Man* proposes a subtle slippage. Once hidden or disembodied, strong or resistant, the male body is neither invisible nor utilitarian. It is vulnerable and fleshy, and to be looked at. Perhaps we can say that *Kikuo* is even male *and* female, or draws qualities from both conventional forms equally. Takano's concern is to challenge the structure and expectations of masculinity: borrowing codes from the representation of femininity in painting, he performs a slippage that crosses mediums and bodies; the question of what reality is, posed by early modern painting, is brought to the photographic image. It is brought to the body also: the body is formed, shaped and brought into being.

Takano is an artist who shows us how to rethink vision. He tests the capacities of photography, playfully, subversively. His use of photography is not to show us what we already know, but to show how the world is formed of a continually shifting, displacing vision, a coming into being.

DUNCAN WOOLDRIDGE

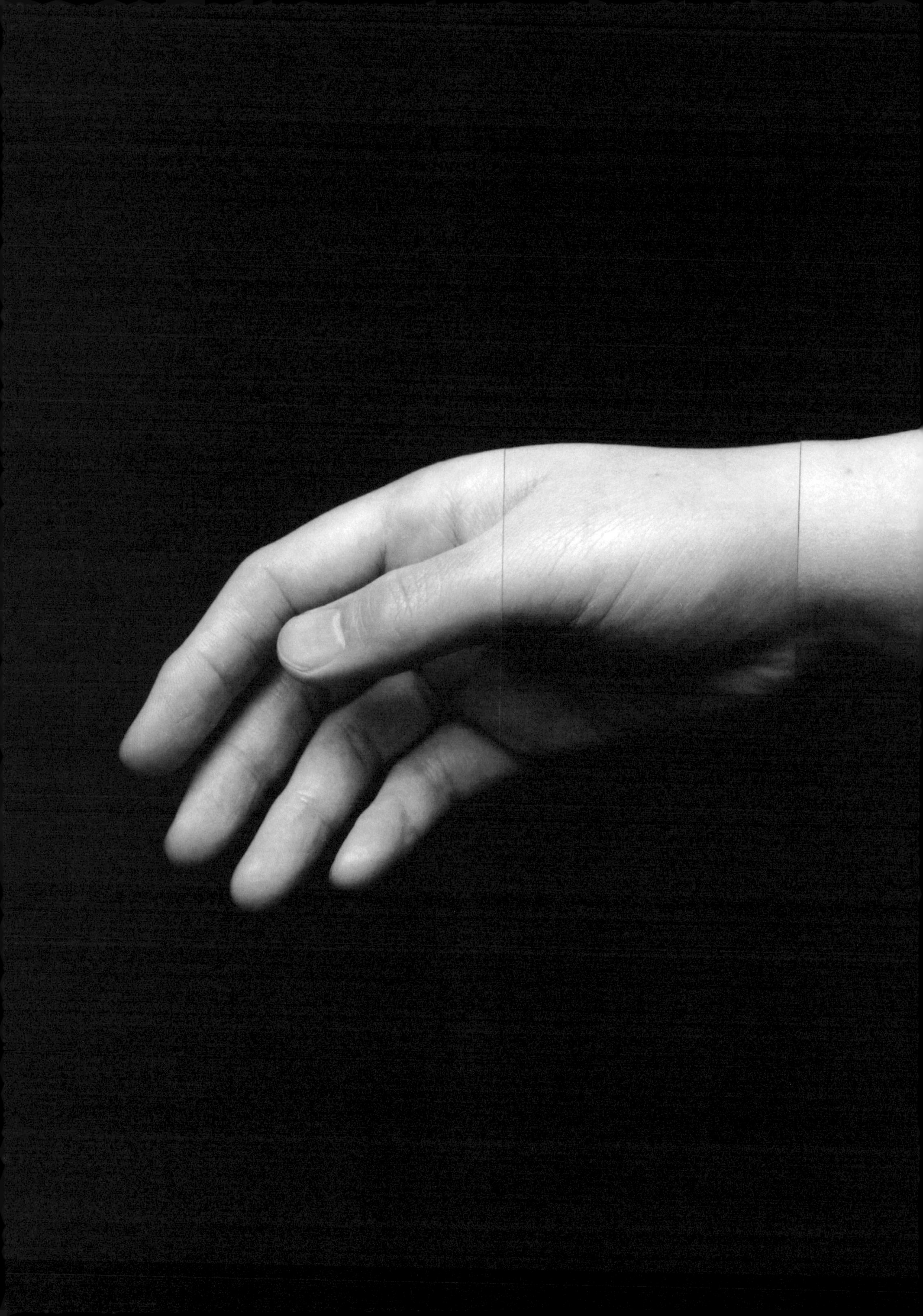

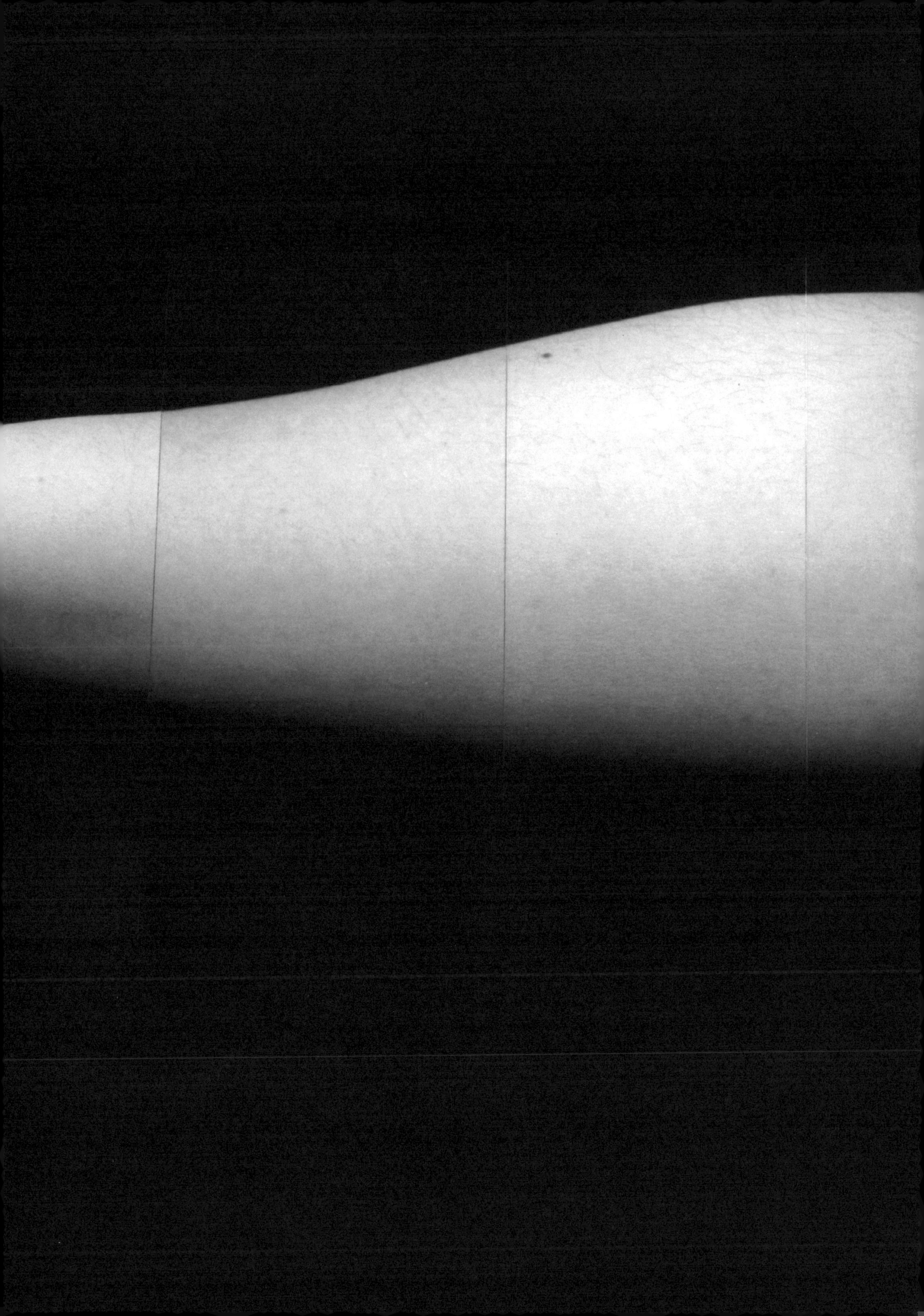

KIKUO (1999.09.17.L.#05)
(RECLINING WOO-MAN), 1999

PREVIOUS SPREAD:
HB#19
(HUMAN BODY I/I), 1999

FOLLOWING SPREAD:
KIKUO (1999.09.17.L.#11)
(RECLINING WOO-MAN), 1999

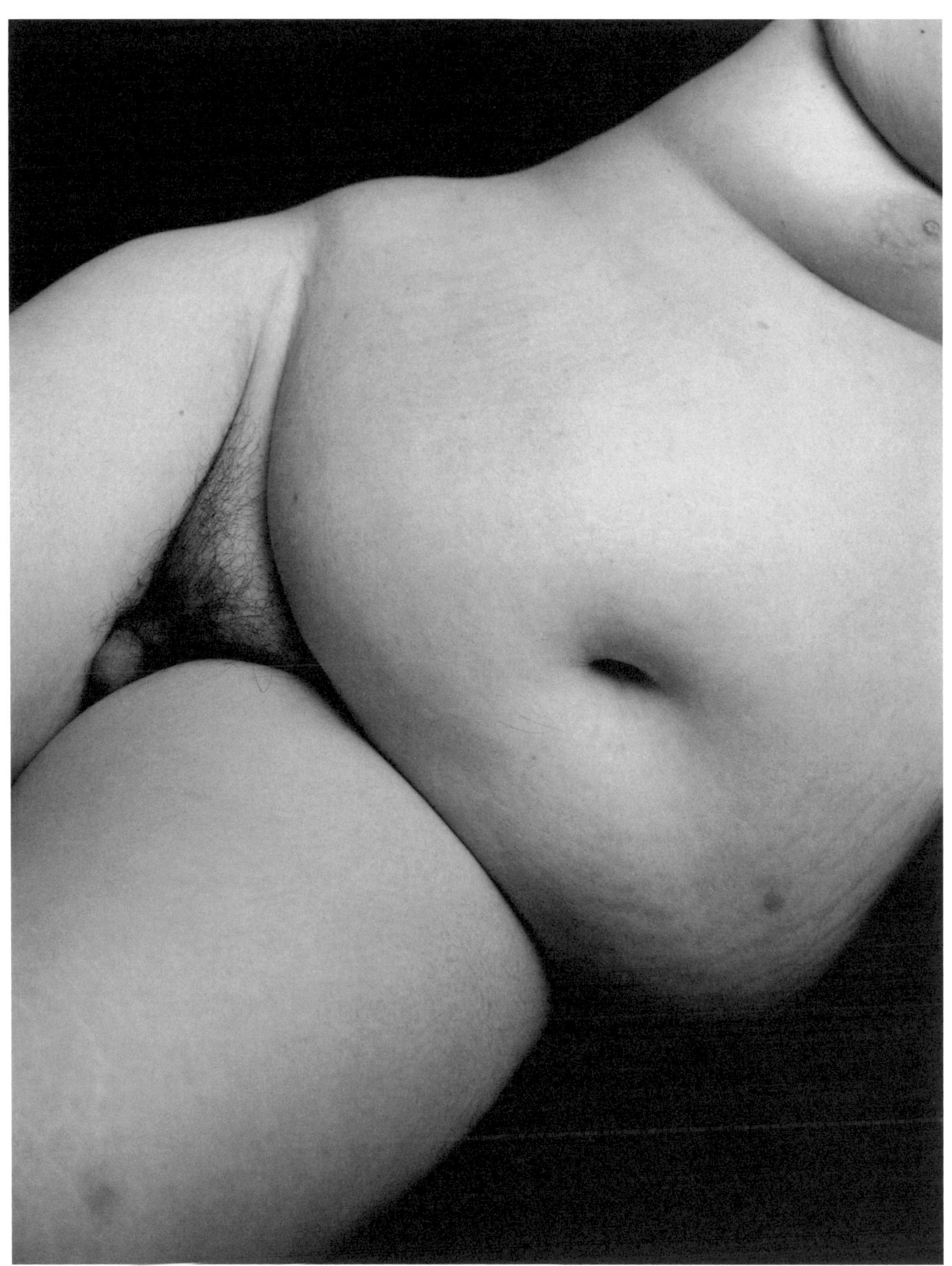

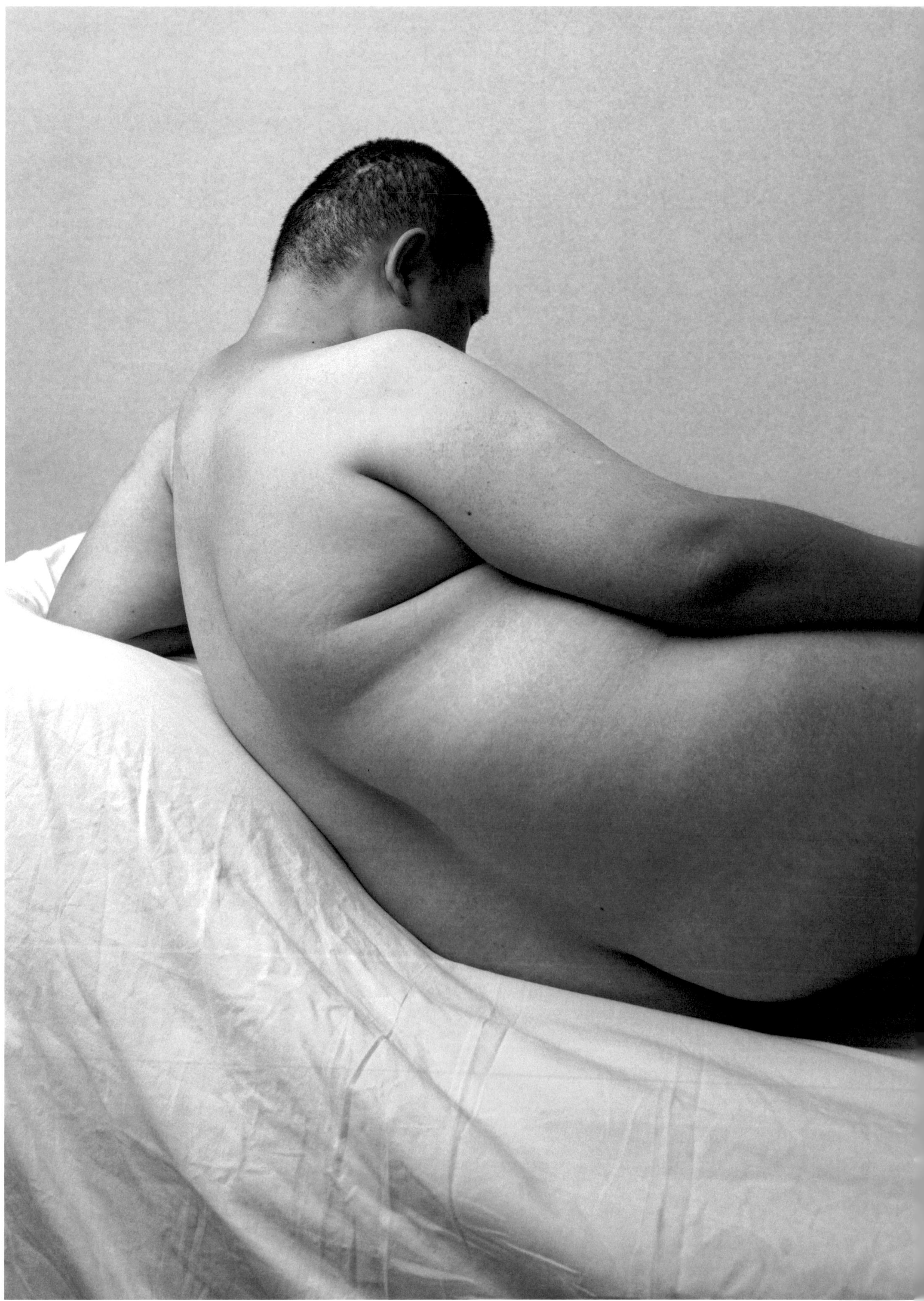

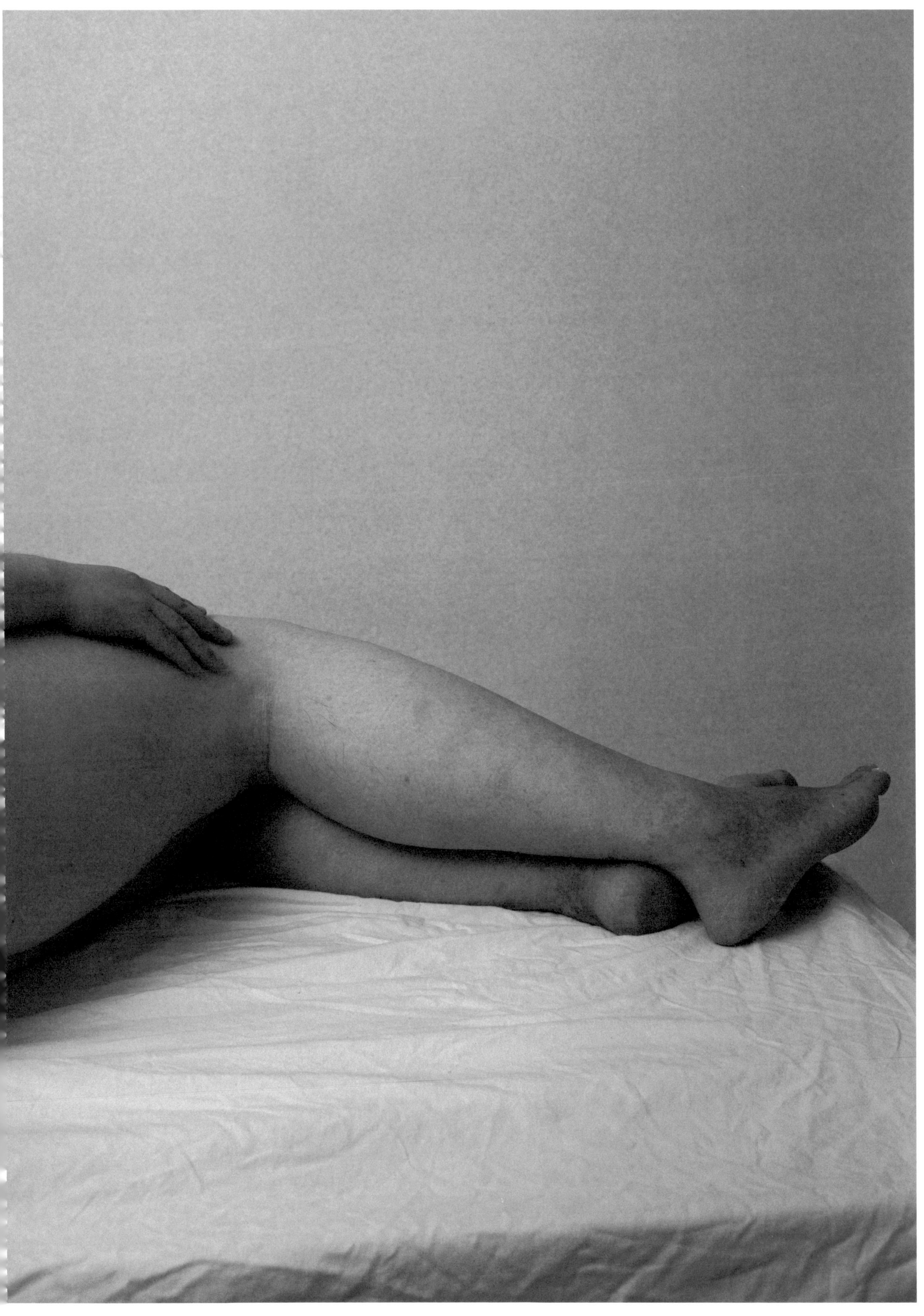

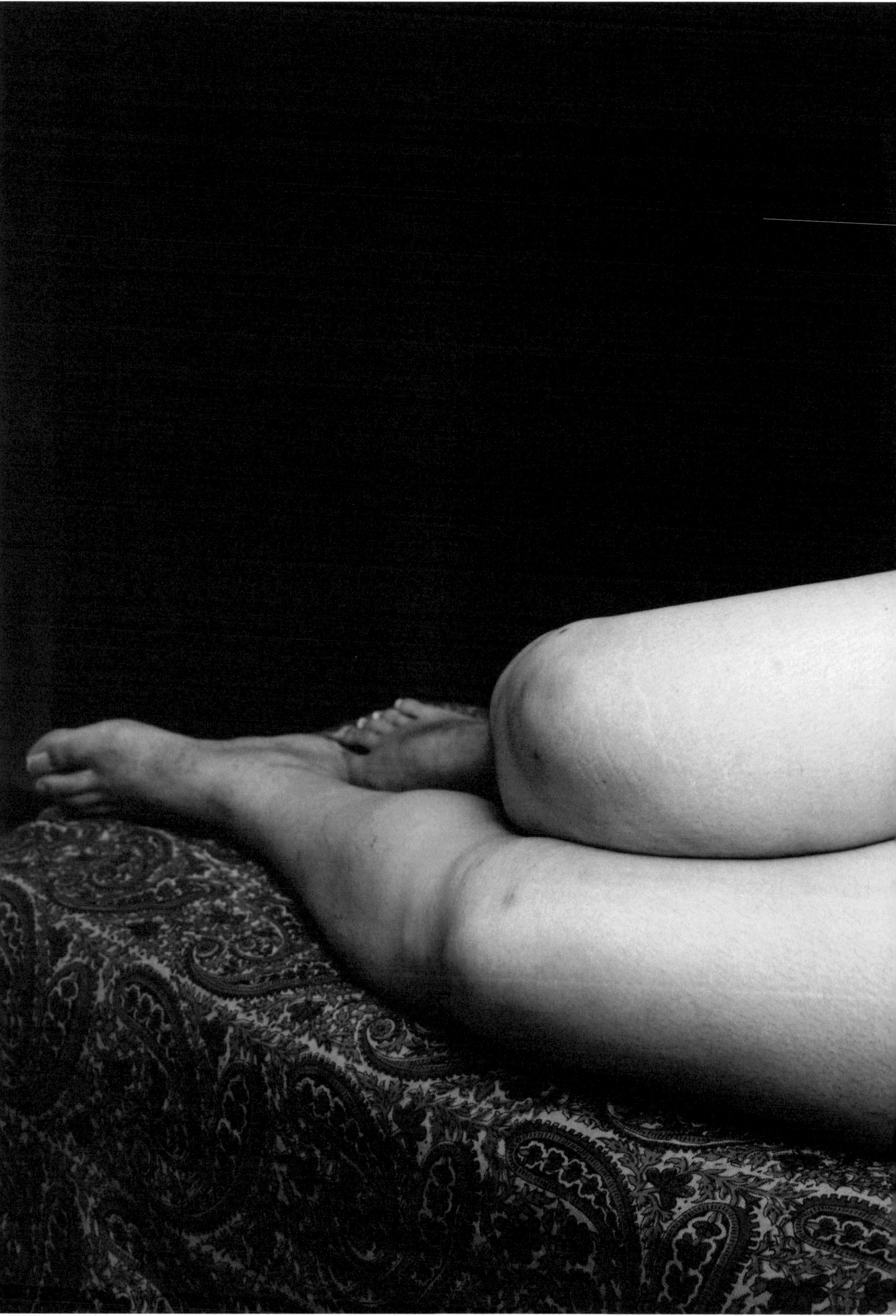

KIKUO (1999.09.17.L.#02)
(RECLINING WOO—MAN), 1999

KIKUO (1999.09.17.L.#02)
(RECLINING WOO—MAN), 1999

FOLLOWING SPREAD:
KIKUO (1999.09.17.L.#16)
(RECLINING WOO—MAN), 1999

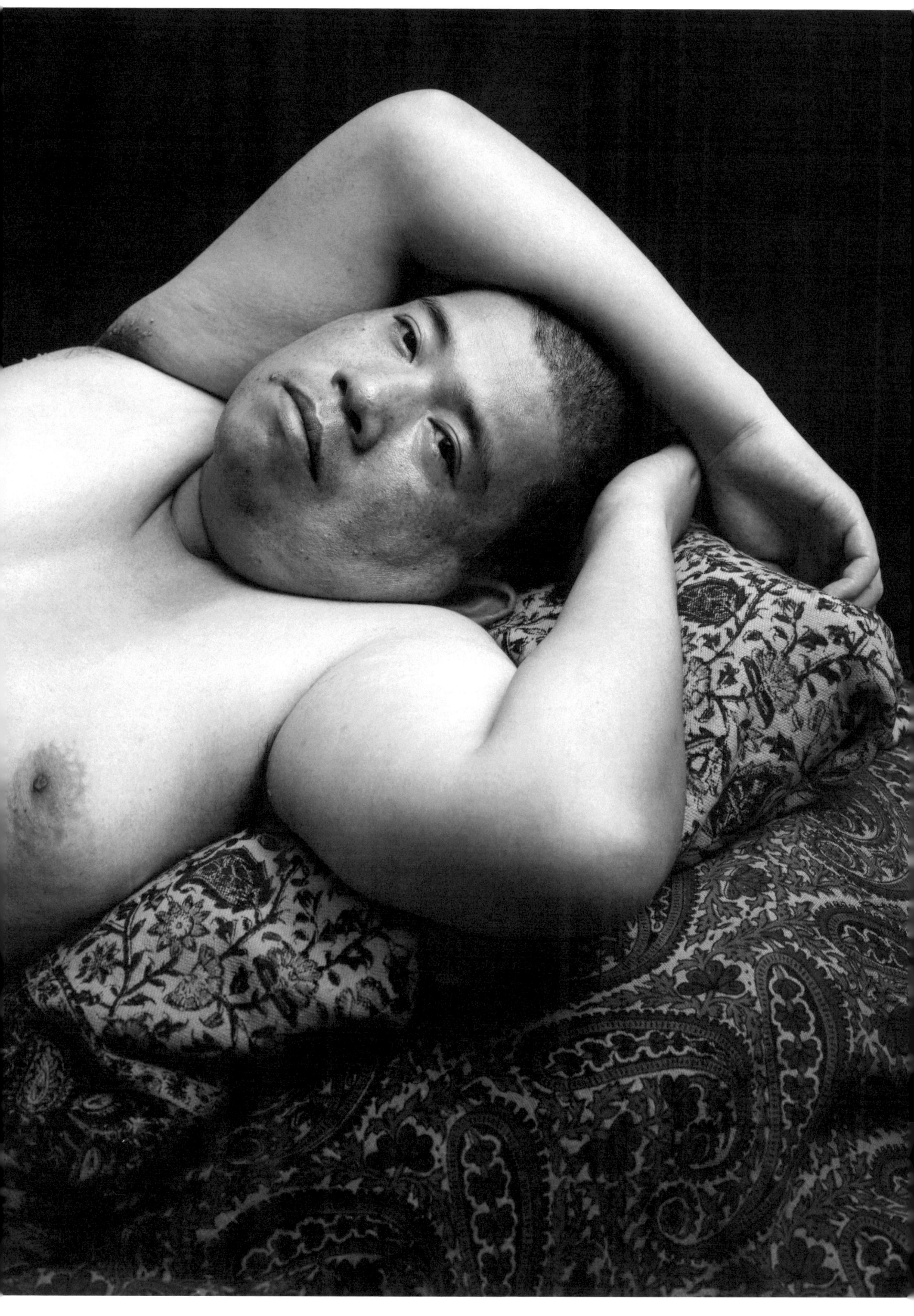

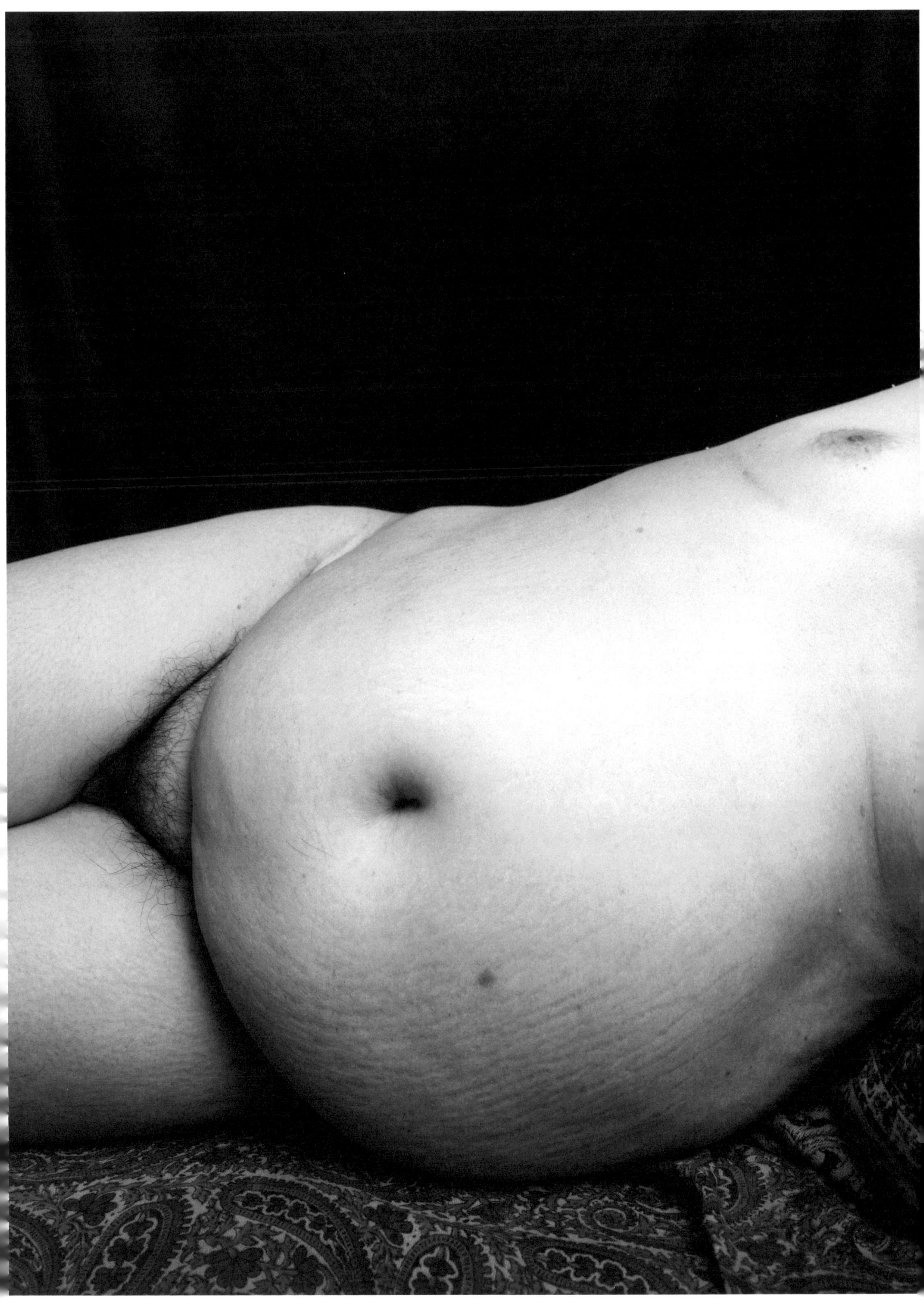

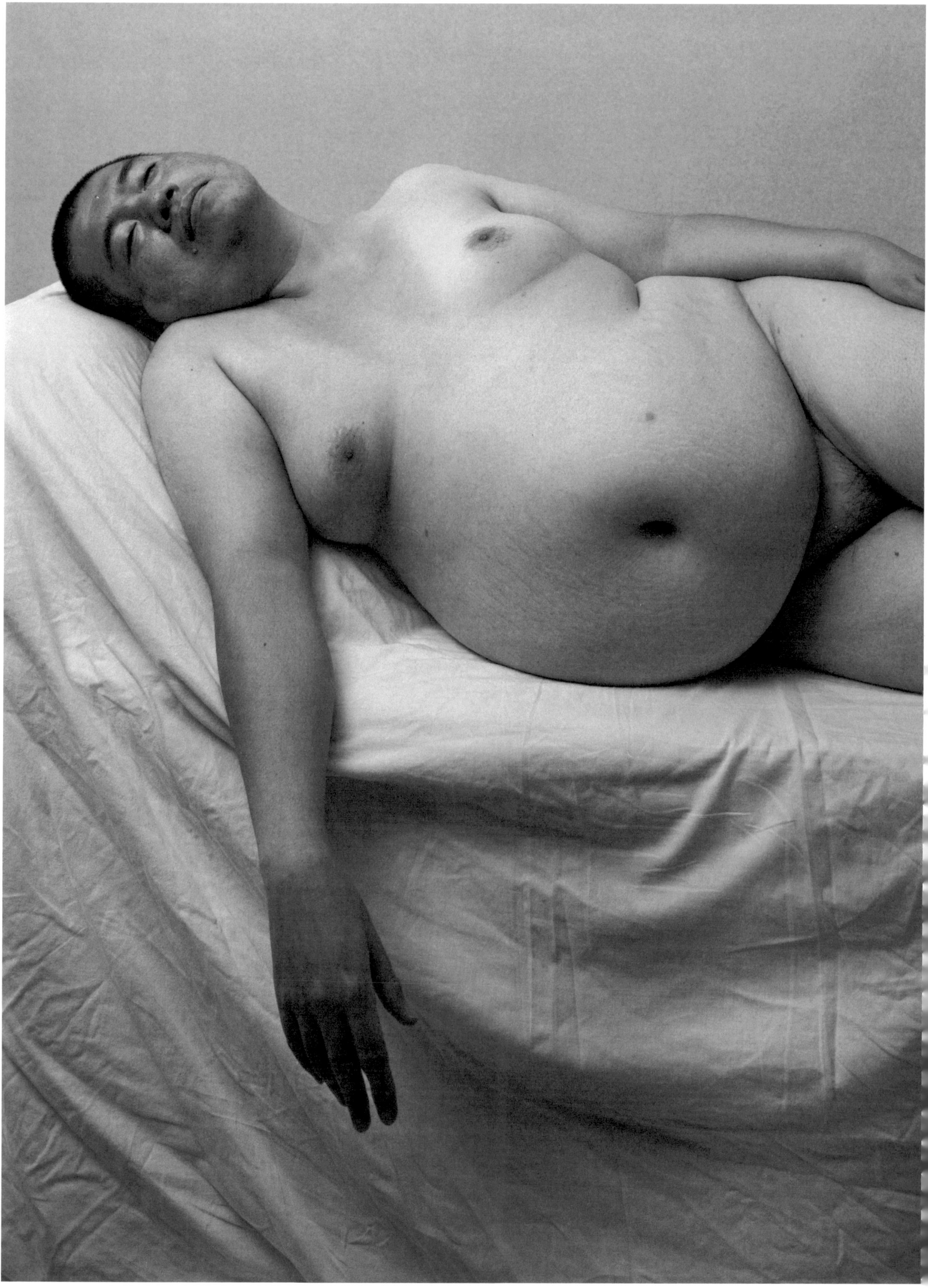

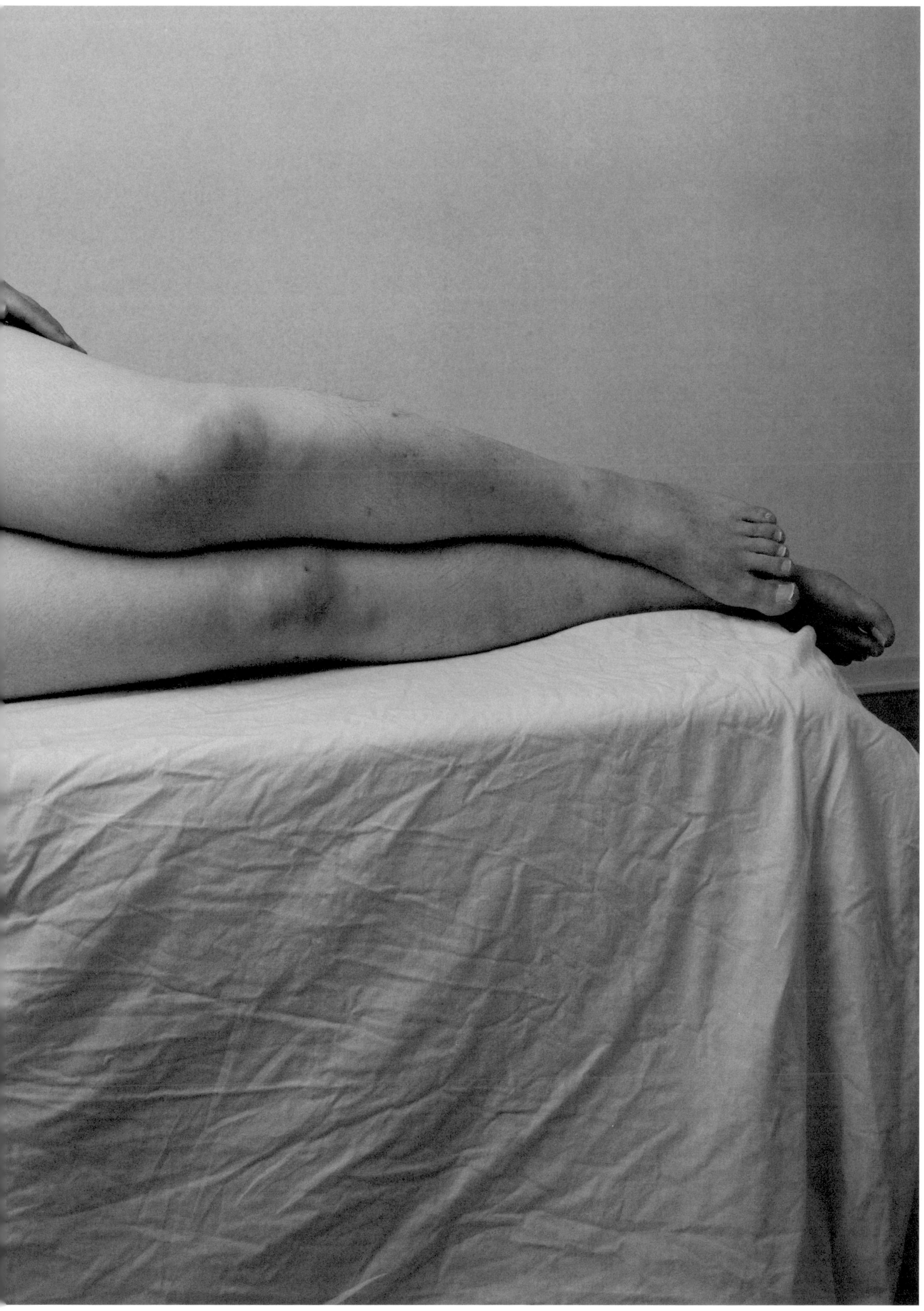

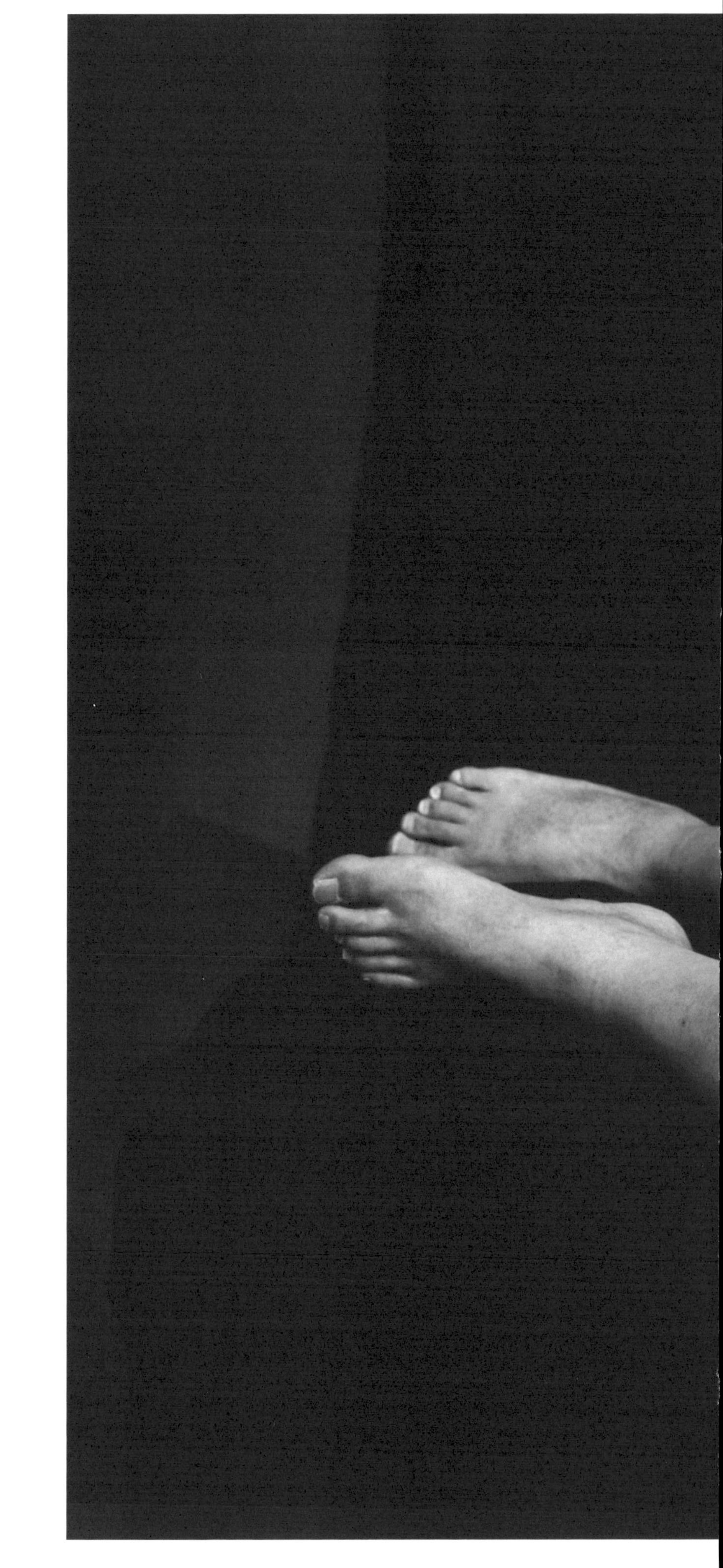

KIKUO (1999.09.17.L.#04)
(RECLINING WOO—MAN), 1999

FOLLOWING SPREAD:
KIKUO (1999.09.17.L.#14)
(RECLINING WOO—MAN), 1999

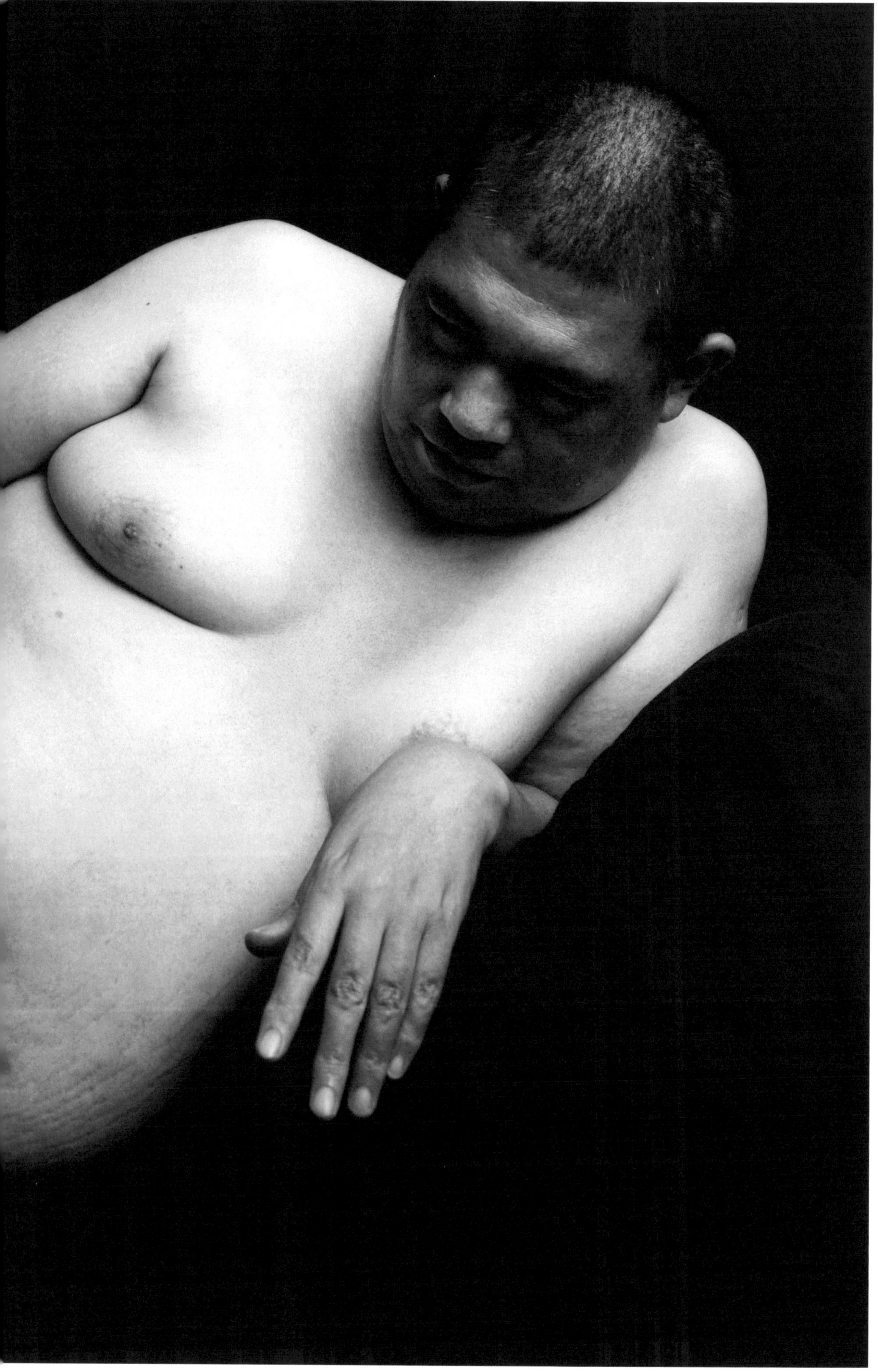

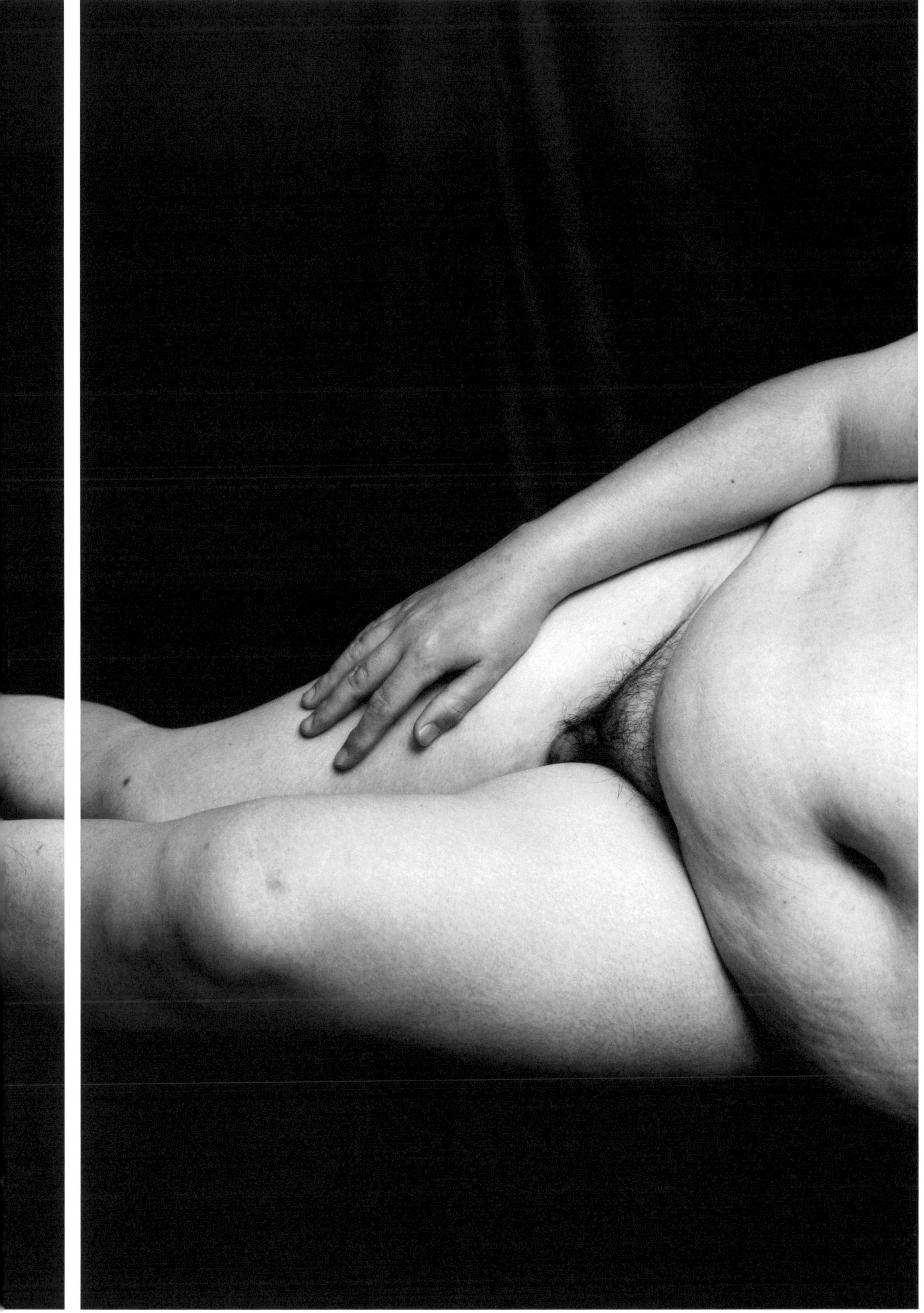

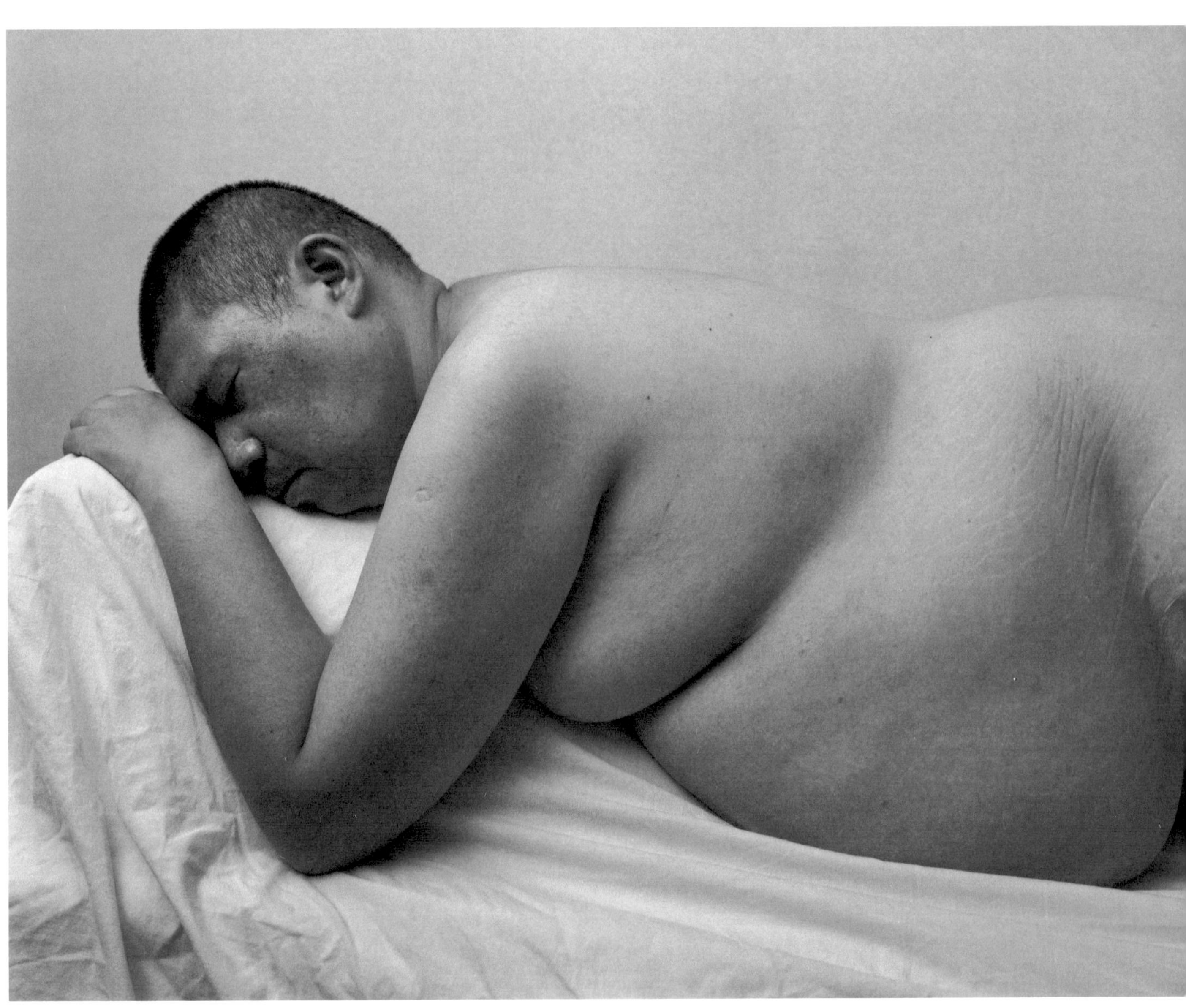

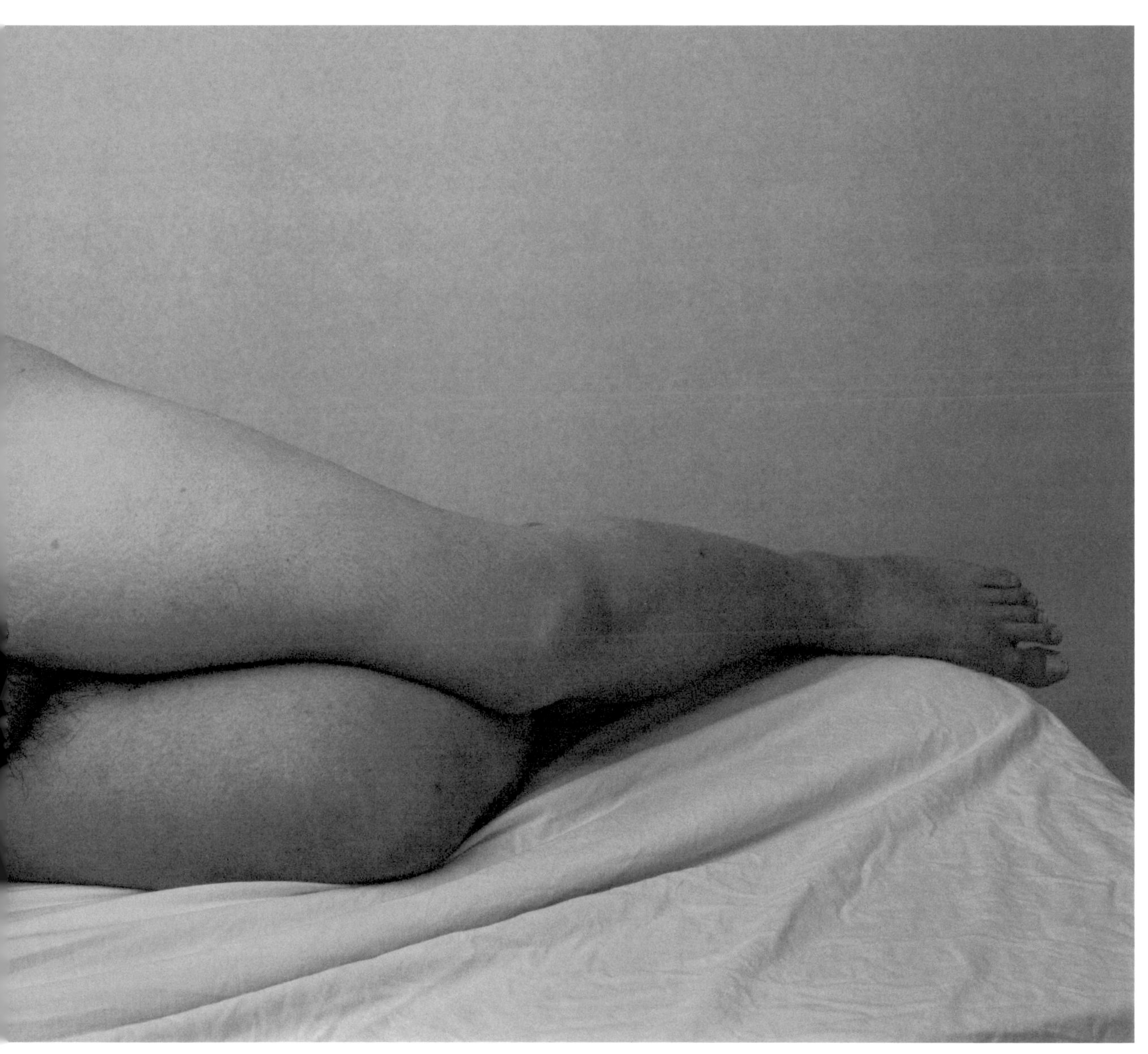

KIKUO (RECLINING WOO-MAN) by Ryudai Takano is printed in a
first edition of five hundred copies. The first thirty copies are numbered
and come as a special edition, each containing an original print, signed and
numbered by the author. Choice of two prints—fifteen copies of each print.

Published in Stockholm, Sweden by Libraryman. Edited and designed in
Antwerp, Belgium by Tony Cederteg. Prepress and printing in Gothenburg,
Sweden by Göteborgstryckeriet.

This book was made with courtesy of Yumiko Chiba Associates.

The publisher wishes to thank Ibasho Gallery and Yumiko Chiba Associates.

ISBN Libraryman: 978-91-88113-43-6

libraryman.se